T0041843

STOOLS AND BOTTLES

STOOLS AND BOTTLES

by The Author of

THE LITTLE RED BOOK

A STUDY OF
CHARACTER DEFECTS
●
31 DAILY MEDITATIONS

Hazelden
Publishing

ISBN 978-0-89486-027-0

Printed and Manufactured in the
United States of America

DEDICATION

This book is humbly dedicated to the members of Alcoholics Anonymous. Its purpose is to stimulate interest in the daily application of the A.A. program by which we arrest our alcoholism. May it help each member and render a special service to the newcomer to whom we are ever obligated to carry the message of the Twelve Steps.

AUTHOR'S NOTE

Some years ago the author of *The Little Red Book* worked out a novel presentation of the first four steps of the A.A. program. Visual aids, consisting of a three-legged stool and eight empty whiskey bottles, were used to portray the intangible factors of these fundamental steps.

The three legs of the stool illustrated Steps 1-2-3. The bottles graphically depicted the character defects revealed by Step 4. Later this became known as the "Stool and Bottle Talk."

This talk proved so helpful to alcoholics in all stages of recovery that many groups asked that it be presented to their membership at special meetings. These requests were frequently granted, but it was impossible to meet most of them. Lack of time and money curtailed them to a great extent.

Members claimed cumulative benefits from these meetings. Visually impressed with the principles of Steps 1-2-3-4, they improved upon their daily use.

Invariably, duplicate sets of bottles and reprints of the talk were requested. Because the talk was extemporaneous, and the bottles too costly, all of these requests could not be met.

But now it is possible to give the highlights of the talk, and to present the "Stools and Bottles" in this book which bears their name. Study groups may find the matter helpful.

To meet our need for quiet periods of thought and prayer, the book provides thirty-one daily reminders. They deal with A.A. problems commonly encountered by alcoholics who try to make A.A. their way of life.

STUDY SUGGESTIONS

We strongly urge every new member to own and study the books *Alcoholics Anonymous* and the *Twelve Steps and Twelve Traditions*. In them we find the answers to our many alcoholic problems. They can be secured from A.A. World Services, Inc., P.O. Box 459, Grand Central Station, New York, N. Y. 10017.

Members who wish to complete their study of the mechanics of the 12 Steps, started in this book, will find them discussed in *The Little Red Book*.

It explains the working principles of each step in greater detail than we have attempted to interpret them, with little duplication of the matter presented here. Copies are available from Hazelden, Center City, Minnesota 55012.

ACKNOWLEDGMENTS

The issues in *Stools and Bottles* could not have been presented without the helpful guidance and constructive criticism of many A.A. members during its preparation.

These people are in no way responsible for errors in judgment and interpretation of the matters discussed in this book. Where error exists it reflects upon the judgment and fallibility of the author only.

Special thanks and appreciation go to Alcoholics Anonymous Publishing, Inc., for their approval to quote from the 12 Steps of A.A. Grateful acknowledgment is also made for their permission to reprint the "Twelve Steps and Twelve Traditions" in the text of this book.

Full appreciation is expressed to Mr. Bennett Cerf for the story of the lumberjack taken from his Ban-

tam book, *Anything for a Laugh.*
Its analogy has helped us to accentuate the alcoholic's inability to profit from past experience.

E. A. W.

CONTENTS

11

CONTENTS *(continued)*

A. A. MAGNET

The Creator's natural laws are put to such common use these days that we accept them without question. Beyond expecting them to work, we give them but little thought or appreciation.

It was under these circumstances that I stood one day watching a giant crane transfer scrap steel from a huge pile to a car which was being loaded.

The crane lifted the steel by means of a large electric magnet. Trip after trip was made from the pile to the car, never varying in its procedure. Every time the current was applied the steel nearest the magnet jumped into contact with it. Other nearby pieces were attracted,

13

but being insecurely attached rose up, dangled momentarily in mid-air, and then fell back onto the pile. The magnet often caught them upon its return trip, but not always. Sometimes it would be several trips later.

Finally, the scrap was deposited in the car and hauled to the foundry to be melted down and recast into new castings. Observing that a small pile of metal still remained on the ground, I appeased my curiosity by investigating the cause. The remaining pieces were of non-ferrous metal which is immune to the power of magnetic force.

Meditating upon man's willing acceptance of laws governing the powers of nature, I marveled at his reluctance to more fully utilize the forces of spiritual power and energy.

In pensive mood, my thoughts turned to A.A. and how a Higher Power seemed to work through it, like a *great spiritual magnet*; how some members with good spiritual contacts are returned to health and sanity; how others, insulated with reservation, finally slide back into their old drinking habits, but how later they make their contact and are recovered, too.

In a moment of real appreciation, I thanked God for A.A. and the miracles performed through it. I asked His help "to carry the message" to those who were ready and to be more tolerant of those who had refused it.

It is in this humble spirit of service that the *Twelve Steps and Twelve Traditions** are quoted, for they are the principles under which the groups live and by which they operate.

*This Book available from A.A. World Service, Inc., P.O. Box 459, New York, N.Y. 10017

15

"THE TWELVE STEPS"

STEP ONE—*"We admitted we were powerless over alcohol — that our lives had become unmanageable."*

STEP TWO — *"Came to believe that a Power greater than ourselves could restore us to sanity."*

STEP THREE — *"Made a decision to turn our will and our lives over to the care of God as we understood Him."*

STEP FOUR — *"Made a searching and fearless moral inventory of ourselves."*

STEP FIVE—*"Admitted to God, to ourselves and to another human being the exact nature of our wrongs."*

STEP SIX — *"Were entirely ready to have God remove all these defects of character."*

STEP SEVEN — *"Humbly asked Him to remove our shortcomings."*

STEP EIGHT — *"Made a list of*

16

all persons we had harmed, and became willing to make amends to them all."

STEP NINE — *"Made direct amends to such people wherever possible, except when to do so would injure them or others."*

STEP TEN — *"Continued to take personal inventory and when we were wrong promptly admitted it."*

STEP ELEVEN—*"Sought through prayer and meditation to improve our conscious contact with God as we understood Him, praying only for knowledge of His will for us and the power to carry that out."*

STEP TWELVE — *"Having had a spiritual awakening as the result of those steps, we tried to carry this message to alcoholics and to practice these principles in all our affairs."*

The Twelve Steps are found on pages 71 and 72 in the first edition Alcoholics Anonymous *and pages 59 and 60 in the second edition.*

"THE TWELVE TRADITIONS"

TRADITION ONE — *"Our common welfare should come first; personal recovery depends upon A.A. unity."*

TRADITION TWO — *"For our group purpose there is but one ultimate authority—a loving God as He may express Himself in our group conscience. Our leaders are but trusted servants—they do not govern."*

TRADITION THREE — *"The only requirement for A.A. membership is a desire to stop drinking."*

TRADITION FOUR — *"Each group should be autonomous except in matters affecting other groups or A.A. as a whole."*

TRADITION FIVE—*"Each group has but one primary purpose — to carry its message to the alcoholic who still suffers."*

TRADITION SIX — *"An A.A. group ought never endorse, finance or lend the A.A. name to any related facility or outside enterprise lest problems of money, property and prestige divert us from our primary spiritual aim."*

TRADITION SEVEN — *"Every A.A. group ought to be fully self-supporting, declining outside contributions."*

TRADITION EIGHT—*"Alcoholics Anonymous should forever remain nonprofessional, but our service centers may employ special workers."*

TRADITION NINE — *"A.A., as such, ought never be organized; but we may create service boards or committees directly responsible to those they serve."*

TRADITION TEN — *"Alcoholics Anonymous has no opinion on outside issues; hence the A.A. name ought never be drawn into public controversy."*

TRADITION ELEVEN — *"Our public relations policy is based on attraction rather than promotion; we need always maintain personal anonymity at the level of press, radio and films."*

TRADITION TWELVE—*"Anonymity is the spiritual foundation of all our Traditions, ever reminding us to place principles above personalities."*

The Twelve Traditions are to be found on Page 564, in the book, Alcoholics Anonymous.

THE SEAT OF A THREE LEGGED STOOL

Stools without legs would be hard to visualize, or understand, except by a group of alcoholics to whom unusual sights are no great rarity. Being alcoholic ourselves, we boldly present the seat of this stool from which we hope to develop an object lesson and to point out the continuity and close relation between Steps 1-2-3.

The true origin of the three-legged stool has long been lost in antiquity. But we gratefully accept it as it came to us with a single seat, three legs and no back. Can you imagine the modern bar without it?

The legless seat depicted here is as useless, incomplete and undependable as the shaky alcoholic it

21

upholds — the fellow whom psychiatrists claim "has both feet firmly planted in thin air."

Like the seat, we alcoholics must have legs to support us. Our lives are confused, out of balance, uncontrolled. We should no longer deceive ourselves. We have no tolerance for alcohol. Our physical, mental and spiritual legs are gone. We need new ones — the A.A. kind which are suggested by Steps 1-2-3.

STEP ONE

"We admitted we were powerless over alcohol — that our lives had become unmanageable."

What is the lesson of Step One? What message does it bring? Does it assure our recovery when we admit its teachings? What happens if we don't? Is it a humble, honest step? What about this one-legged stool? Of what use is it in A.A.? It has no use — except to illustrate its uselessness. By comparison, each newcomer in A.A. is quite as unbalanced as a one-legged stool, until he adds the other legs. Steps 1-2-3 are A.A.'s basic steps. Like the legs of a stool, they work only as a unit. We need all of them. One will not do the trick any more than one drink would satisfy us in our drinking days.

Stools and Bottles

Now that we are in A.A. and wish to rehabilitate our lives, how do we go about it? Can we learn to control our drinking? If alcoholism is a disease, how is it cured? Where will we find the answers to our many problems?

The answers are given in the book *Alcoholics Anonymous*. Alcoholism is an incurable illness. From the standpoint of control, we can never drink normally again. We can arrest it, however, by living the 12 Steps of A.A. to the best of our ability.

This requires study, patience and practice, but it works! We profit most from first learning the whole truth about ourselves, the alcoholic selves we are, rather than the indispensable individuals whom we think we are. The greatest hurdle we must clear is *self* before we can recover from alcoholism.

This is equally true of our physical, mental and spiritual recovery. For, until we fully concede that our uncontrolled use of alcohol has made us ill we will find no reason for treatment of this illness.

Because our alcoholism is self-inflicted and develops so slowly, we are averse to look upon it as a disease. Thus we retard our recovery with egotistical thoughts of false security.

It is advisable to check our reaction toward practice of the various Steps. When we rebel against the provisions of a Step, we should back away and give that Step close study. The suggestions we rebel against are often the very things we should be doing.

Most sick persons require exacting care. They rarely ask a surgeon to partially remove a malignant growth. That doesn't make sense. Yet many alcoholics come into A.A.

seeking temporary relief from alcoholism which can become as serious as any malignant disease. A realistic view toward alcoholism is our first step toward recovery.

Before A.A., we were always unreliable—drunk or sober. Sober, we might get drunk, and drunk we might do most anything. But nothing we did seemed to make good sense.

We considered alcohol a requisite of life. Mistaking this depressive drug for a stimulant, we progressively became ill from its use. We tried to recapture the old glow and warmth which alcohol once gave. Blind to our addiction, we failed to realize that sooner or later depressive drugs must bring pain instead of pleasure; that the end of our drinking is insanity or alcoholic death. Note — *the latter is entirely physical and decidedly final.*

Unwittingly, we have formed

many harmful physical habits. Admitting them is the first honest thing A.A. asks us to do. It is the only thing we can do. Step 1 suggests that we do it. Its purpose is to convince us that we have become alcoholic. Other Steps of our program will explain how we recover.

Paradoxically, admission of our weakness soon becomes a source of new strength. Make it now and avoid the future reservations that bar success.

Some members, still dishonest with themselves, will not admit their alcoholism. So with closed and belligerent minds they must continue to view sobriety through the cloudy windows of self-centered, alcoholic reservation.

Let's stop resisting recovery and make a true evaluation of Step 1 as it relates to the physical illness of alcoholism. This is clearly explained in paragraphs 1-2-3, pages 2 and 3, in the first edition of *Alcoholics Anonymous* and on page 24. "The Doctor's Opinion", in the second edition. Study these pages.

Many A.A. failures would not have happened had the newcomer been reading his Big Book and realized the importance of good health to his recovery. The toxic, alcoholic poisoning which we have built up within our bodies is not conducive to good health or manageable living. Upon entering A.A. we should make every effort to improve our physical condition, thus qualifying ourselves for the mental and spiritual progress which we hope to make later.

Occasionally we encounter persons who discount the physical illness of alcoholism, claiming it is unimportant. Don't be deceived. We cannot substitute alcohol for food, vitamins, minerals and relaxation over a long period of years without paying a physical penalty.

Any drug that poisons must do it physically. Alcohol is not a beverage for alcoholics — it is a poison. When we drink it we get sick. Remove the physical illness from alcoholism and there isn't much left. In other words, it would be impossible to become alcoholic without drinking alcohol.

We agree that we are mentally and spiritually ill as well, but physical illness brings most of us into A.A. where we treat "First Things First."

Consider the old adage, "Know the truth and the truth shall set you free." The obvious truth is that we have acquired alcoholism, from which we can recover, but cannot be cured. Our allergy to alcohol is out of control. Contented sobriety is now vital for us.

Stools and Bottles

It takes no more courage to face this reality than to sweat out another hangover. Why not face it and start our recovery now? There is no point in waiting. Our next drunk might prove fatal.

Until we stop ducking this issue, A.A. cannot help us, but by facing it we turn lukewarm desire into grim determination to get well. New faith and hope inspire us — we are on our way.

Step One puts a strong leg in our recovery stool, but since a stool is worthless with one leg, let's turn to Step Two for further help.

STEP TWO

"Came to believe that a Power greater than ourselves could restore us to sanity."

Step Two represents the second leg of our recovery stool which is still incomplete but will stand if propped against something more powerful and stable than itself.

Newcomers in A.A., like the stool, need something more dependable to lean upon than the false promises of alcohol. Like the diabetic, who must use insulin or die, we look to some "Power greater than ourselves" for correction of our absurd drinking behavior. Remember how often it bordered upon outright acts of drunken insanity?

Having reached this crisis in our lives, we will benefit from a frank admission of our need for help from "a Higher Power." Either that, or keep on drinking. Shall we let vanity and reservation spoil this last chance to live sanely and soberly? Why continue to head the world's long list of prize suckers? You know — the ones who will not learn from past experience.

Alcoholics consistently excel in making mistakes but refuse to profit from them. Like the stupid workman in the story, they always come out on the short end of life's bounties.

This fellow got a new job in a saw mill. The foreman took him to a buzz saw and explained its operation. Then, after warning him it was dangerous, he sauntered off. Now alone, the workman, fascinated by the whirling contraption, reached an experimental finger toward it. A second later the finger was cut off. The poor workman let out a cry of pain, and the foreman came rushing up. "What happened?" he cried "Your darned saw cut off my finger," gasped the workman. "What in thunder did you do wrong?" asked the foreman. "Danged if I know," said the workman. "I just touched it like this — ouch, there goes another finger."

It is easy to laugh at the lumberjack and keep right on feeding our own fingers into that alcoholic buzz saw. Some of us get our heads into the saw as well, allowing insanity to end all hopes for future freedom or happiness.

This is strong language but we cannot over emphasize the serious nature of alcoholic thinking or its objective — *to drink at any cost.*

To drink at any cost, with no regard for consequences, reduces to its simplest equation the insanity of alcoholism at work.

33

Stools and Bottles

Our intelligence must mark time, or leave entirely, while we alcoholics overcome every obstacle between us and the next drink.

This obsession sets us apart from normal drinkers who can stop at will. Drinking, we lack the natural instinct of self-preservation which violates the first principle of sanity: namely, *the will to survive*. Surely there is mental illness in alcoholism.

Consider the ghastly mornings after the nights before. Remember those jittery, agonizing hangovers and how they belied the sanity of our drinking? How they kept us in sickening weakness, remorse and fear, until life was void and as unstable as a two-legged stool.

In desperation, we took more alcohol to bolster our enfeebled energy, as our dear ones stood by, vainly trying to help. By the time we had consumed enough alcohol to quiet our jitters, we were drunk again — and obviously insane by anybody's standard.

Sick and distraught, we phoned for more liquor or traveled to a barroom, and in tragic compulsion continued to drink on energy and money we did not possess. Stupefied, we drank without recall into a new day — another hangover.

Among the symptoms of our mental illness are such things as that first drink which starts a new binge, unpredictable behavior, deep resentments, drinking for spite, lack of self-criticism and emotional instability.

Add to this list our other mental quirks and we find additional symptoms of our mental illness. For example: fear—fits of anger—stinking thinking — criticism — dishonesty — delusions — blackouts — D.T.'s — suicide — refusal to admit

35

that we are ill and that we need help.

We need help all right but not the kind we, or any other human being, can render. The second leg of our recovery stool is suggested by Step Two. It is help from "A Power greater than ourselves — to restore us to sanity." Suggestions for this help are taken from a basic law of recovery. It does not fail those who sincerely use it. Having failed· with our own power, perhaps we can regain our sanity from faith in a Higher Power. Others have done it.

Being convinced of this, it seems advisable to consider Step Three — the third leg of our recovery stool.

STEP THREE

"Made a decision to turn our will and our lives over to the care of God as we understood Him."

Step Three puts the last leg on our recovery stool which now stands solidly upon three strong legs, ready for useful service.

It brings us face to face with the thing we have long avoided — a standard for spiritual living. A rough standard for those who are not ready, but a real lifesaver for those who are.

Step Three is just as important to successful recovery from alcoholism as the third leg is to our stool. We need spiritual help to recover. Without it we have little more than unhappy sobriety, often not even that.

37

Stools and Bottles

This becomes apparent to those who are ready for A.A., but it is a mystery to those who are not. Being unwilling to regard alcoholism as an incurable malady (physical — mental — spiritual), they seek a cure for this incurable illness. Not realizing that admission of their illness is the first requisite of recovery, they face future trouble.

Borrowing this thought from *The Little Red Book*,* we are reminded that "The first three steps are a composite A.A. package. Conceived in meditation and experience, they are a basic recovery prescription, and when taken with proper timing and in correct proportion, they quickly arrest our alcoholic condition. Complementing each other, however, they fail to work if any one of them is omitted."

*The Little Red Book *is available from your group secretary or Hazelden, Center City, Minnesota 55012.*

To agree with this theory is much easier than to live it. Lip service gets us nowhere. Successful A.A. members are those who sacrifice their reservations upon the altar of sobriety and lose themselves in 12 Step living.

There is certain spiritual illness in alcoholism. Step Three gives a solution for its treatment. This is a simple solution, yet for some it is quite difficult. Its success lies in our willingness to discipline our minds with spiritual thinking. Indifference and prejudice are the chief barriers to success. Alcoholic minds rebel against the surrender which this step suggests.

Our decision to enter A.A. was not made with the knowledge that it would be a spiritual way of life. A.A.'s help and understanding are welcome, but Step Three has a familiar ring — it smacks of religion and some do not like it. They ask, "Is A.A. a religion?" Our answer is "No, it is a 24-hour recovery program borrowed from medicine, psychology and religion—a daily way of life by which we arrest alcoholism."

Before deciding against the logic of A.A.'s spiritual benefit, why not first consider our reasons for being here? Are we here to rebel or recover? To rewrite the 12 Steps, or to live them? To make fools of over four hundred thousand alcoholics who recovered by them, or to try and recover too? Dare we pass up our only source of help left? Yes, we can if we wish. But that is hardly consistent with our A.A. purpose.

Our aversion to spiritual law is a good example of alcoholic inconsistency. We accept the Creator's natural laws without question, but reject the spiritual laws necessary to recovery. What is our reason? Why do we accept God's physical laws and lack the faith to benefit from spiritual help?

Few of us believe that at sundown the sun will never rise again, or that the earth, moon, stars and other terrestrial bodies will cease revolving in their orbits. Our faith in their performance is unlimited.

There are no grounds for doubting the law of gravity. We believe in it. We can't defy it. Elevators prove this contention and are still used to descend from the top floors of high buildings. This practice will probably continue unless some alcoholic discovers how to disprove it. The law of gravity discourages faster methods of descent, such as jumping down elevator shafts or leaping out of windows.

Oddly enough, though, this does happen to some who persist in violating God's physical, mental and spiritual laws. Not all leap out of windows. Some pay penalties in other ways, but there are penalties to be paid and drinking alcoholics pay them, one way or another.

On the other hand, there are many rewards for spiritual living. To be quite definite about the matter, they outnumber the penalties and should be good reasons for accepting Step Three.

By the daily spiritual practices of A.A., we lift ourselves out of the depths of alcoholic weakness and ignorance to strength, health and a new understanding of our purpose in life.

The 12 Steps teach us how to exchange old goods for new. Daily we trade fear for courage, drunkenness for sobriety, and despair for assurance.

Members are often reluctant to

use the new source of power which Step 3 opens up for them. We should use it. It is a source of power which will assure us sobriety and peace of mind. We always rise above our problems when we resign our reservations to God's Will.

These are the satisfying results of spiritual living. These are the rewards to be gained from surrender of our will to that of a Higher Power. It is not hard to do, or too difficult to understand, providing we have been hurt enough and are determined to stop at nothing short of recovery.

Nobody tells us how we shall live the program or how we must understand God. That is our privilege. But we can draw helpful conclusions from the experiences of successful older members who are ready and willing to help us. The purpose of this discussion is directed toward that end.

Since there will be as many interpretations of God as there are members in A.A., no fixed plan of action can be given. But it is obvious that studying the 12 Steps and asking God's Will daily should be most helpful.

Step Three covers a lot of territory and, at times, becomes confusing. We will avoid confusion by first dividing the step into three parts, with a view of studying each part separately. Later putting them together, we learn how they function as a whole.

This allows us to see the actual working mechanics of the Step and lessens our tendencies toward a biased or emotional acceptance of it. Thus we avoid confusion and reduce spiritual prejudice by presenting the matter so that each member may form his own concept of a Higher Power. It is important that we have this concept as A.A. teaches that our recovery from alcoholism "is contingent upon our spiritual condition."

A caution should be observed at this point. It may challenge our openmindedness and test our willingness to accept and enlarge upon A.A.'s spiritual possibilities. For, although we may have strong convictions, either for God or against Him, the fact remains they were powerless against alcoholism. Our unmanageable lives proved that.

It is evident that open-mindedness is necessary to our plan of recovery. We will have to change much self-centered thinking and kill those ideas about the 12 Step program which tend to defeat its purpose. It is easy to get lopsided ideas regarding its principles. Some ideas are pretty cock-eyed, yet we all had them. Newcomers

45

will continue to have them but will finally lose them the same as we did.

For this reason, we must be tolerant with each other, ever trying to help one another with as much understanding and consideration as possible.

Steps 1 and 2 have identified an incurable illness in our lives. Step 3 suggests a proved, effective treatment for the spiritual part of this illness. This step has three proposals which, as explained, will be studied separately.

"MADE A DECISION"

Upon what grounds shall this decision be made? Illness or idiosyncrasies? Members have failed in A.A. because of the latter. Too impatient to "carry the message" and to advance their fellowship status, they soon leap over the decision in Step 3, looking for new worlds to conquer. Poor progress follows as they never conquor nor enrich their minds with 12 Step understanding.

Like people traveling without road maps, they generally arrive at the wrong places. Compliance takes the place of surrender and trouble begins. For them, alcoholism is but lack of will power, or perhaps, just plain sin. Recovery under such conditions is unpredictable. For until we truly face our real problems and are willing to overcome all of them, we can expect little help from A.A.

What are some of these conditions?

What do alcoholics substitute for their actual problems? Who fails in A.A.? Why?

1. Those who look upon alcoholism as a moral problem rather than an incurable disease.

47

2. Reluctant members forced into A.A. to keep out of the "dog house."

3. Members who join up just for the ride — strictly "on the wagon" — hogging the "driver's seat."

4. Some who are heavy drinkers but not alcoholics.

5. Alcoholics, but constitutionally dishonest.

6. The occasional atheist or agnostic who will not accept a spiritual program such as ours.

7. Members whose A.A. purpose is publicity and personal gain.

8. Alcoholics who would dry up for the good of others.

9. Newcomers in A.A. to appease other people — like wives, husbands, judges, employers, rela-

tives, business associates and friends.

10. Members with reservations. The boys and gals who accept only parts of the 12 Steps — upon which they place a distorted interpretation with self-centered intent.

It is true that many good resolutions might arise from the various reasons listed, but they would not keep us from drinking long. No reason will until it includes alcoholism — fatal and incurable. Others fall short of the mark and give no reason for a far-reaching decision such as that required by Step Three.

The crux of this step is the decision. Read it over. Does it ask for anything more? Steps 1 and 2 are the only premise upon which our decisions can honestly be made. Sobriety and peace of mind depend upon the kind of decision we make. Make it serious.

We have all decided upon important matters before, but believe it or not, this is the most important decision we could be called upon to make at this time. Our future welfare and security depend upon it.

Actually, our spiritual possibilities are unlimited when we willingly and honestly decide to live them.

How we carry out the provisions of Step 3 is not a matter of immediate concern. Other Steps in our program tell us how to do this. We will get to them in due time. Nothing is more important to us right now than an intelligent decision to accept this Step without reservations.

By experience we have learned that a decision based upon any reason other than alcoholism will not last. But when based upon alcoholism, an illness (physical—mental — spiritual), it keeps us active in A.A. — sober and contented.

It awakens us to our real need for help and to the nature of that need. We stop kidding ourselves and honestly evaluate our true alcoholic condition. This knowledge creates a strong incentive for accepting Step 3. It supplies a motive for surrender of our alcoholic will to a Power greater than ourselves.

Unless we can find some power that is greater than our own, something more important than alcohol, we have nothing to live for. Why keep on drinking and subjecting our will to John Barleycorn, that sneaky, double-crossing guy who only rewards in despair, insanity and alcoholic death?

This does not infer that sobriety should be gained through fear. On

51

the contrary, we gain it through faith and courage. Fear is a form of ignorance. Faith, based on knowledge, is a sign of intelligence. Fear is not lasting. It leaves us quickly and we start drinking again. Craving a drink, we fear no consequence, which is ample reason for making the decision suggested by Step 3. Armed with it and the truth about our alcoholism, we start our recovery.

We are now at the second division of the step — that part dealing with our will and lives which suggests that we turn them over to the care of God.

To clarify our discussion, we will subdivide the second division, presenting the alcoholic's will first.

TURNING OUR WILL OVER
TO GOD

Having made a decision, our next step is to "turn our will over to the care of God, as we understand Him." At least, that is all we propose to consider at the moment.

The question before us is simple. What is an alcoholic's will? We shall deal with it in all simplicity to avoid the many complexities we would otherwise encounter. The truth is — *We will to drink when and where we choose, resigned to drinking's penalties*. The fact that we have lost the power of choice narrows down the purpose of our will to one choice, namely — to drink.

This flat statement of an alcoholic's will relates to his unpredictable drinking behavior and is open to argument. Few of us drank all of the time. Some members served their communities. Others held responsible positions contributing to the welfare of their families. But only by bluff, lies, imposition and the co-operative support of friends and families did we manage to conduct much important business.

Therein lies the rub, for when the urge to drink came, families, religion and business were neglected and disregarded in favor of drunkenness. We have rationalized this all too long. We're in A.A. now. Let's stop it.

Medicine and psychiatry seek scientific reasons for our drinking. But not A.A. We admit the results, surmounting them with our spiritual way of life. For this reason, we advise new members to remain laymen. Alcoholics do not stay sober who try to become able doctors and clergymen overnight. Knowing that members try it, we stress the tendency so it may be avoided.

The will of the drinking alcoholic seems to point in one direction — toward the bottle. Perhaps we should briefly consider our drinking attitude.

There is no identical pattern of behavior to which alcoholics conform. There is a fixed ratio of binges, however, for those who swear off for certain periods of time. The new binges are always in proportion to the resolutions to stop drinking. That is how the alcoholic will functions.

Even on the wagon, we were never sure just how long we'd be there. We knew exactly the number of days we'd been sober, but had no idea of when we might take that first drink. The exception being, when on a definite period of sobriety, we were counting the days until the next drunk.

We claimed that we wanted to

55

quit drinking. We thought we meant it. We didn't want to quit. We only wished that we wanted to. What we actually wanted was to control our drinking, at least enough to keep out of trouble.

The word trouble has a wide range of meaning for the drinking alcoholic. Physically, it can refer to anything from an upset stomach to an alcoholic death. Between these two extremes we are subject to many other infirmities, all because of our unconscious alcoholic will to drink without restraint.

For example, there is anemia, mineral and vitamin deficiency, big heads, jitters, cold sweats, pneumonia, liver and heart conditions, alcoholic neuritis, low blood sugar, chronic alcoholic poisoning and kindred ailments. The greater the affliction, the more our alcoholic will leans toward the bottle.

Any one, or a combination of these maladies, meant trouble for us. Blackouts, D.T.'s, insanity and other sickness added to our difficulties. They all resulted in mental and bodily discomfort and loss of valuable time. Because of them we often required hospitalization. At times, we sweat them out at home, but not without someone's aid and tolerance or without loss to our business interests.

Trouble presented itself in other forms such as ill health, anxiety and fear. Under alcoholic influence anything might happen, and it always did.

Drunkenness begot drunkenness. It dulled our judgment and finer sensibilities. Financial difficulties appeared. Creditors became bothersome. Sometimes we brawled, landing in jail. At times we were arrested for intoxication, drunken driving or other law infringements. Divorce and sex problems messed up our lives. On occasion our will to drink amounted to an obsession and always ended in trouble.

Despite the extreme gravity of all these problems, we had others as bad if not worse. How about the alcoholics with advanced brain deterioration or those planning suicide, to say nothing of the unfortunates who try it?

The harm drinking caused us was great but small when compared with the irreparable harm done to others. Sometimes it was physical violence to members of our families. Then there were cases of bodily harm and even death, which we inflicted upon people by reason of our drunken, insane acts. This and the inconceivable emotional harm done them can never be completely listed.

So much for the sorry experiences of our alcoholic willfulness and their tragic effect upon the lives of others. These regrettable acts need not recur once we recognize the spiritual illness of alcoholism and seek God's help to arrest it.

We should make this our ambition. But it must become more than a good resolution. Although God honors faith and service, He does not reward wishful thinking. It is only when we make our lives a channel for His Will that He grants us contented sobriety. His Will regenerates us. Our will to drink can only destroy us.

Sometimes we attribute our alcoholism to sinfulness and a weak will. Gluttony is always sinful, but there is nothing weak about our will to drink.

On the contrary, we were unusually strong willed wherever alcohol

59

was concerned. Not understanding our willfulness, we mistook it for weakness. Our conscious mind often prompted us to put on the brakes, so we made sober resolutions. For indefinite periods they gave a restive, water wagon kind of sobriety. But deep within, buried in our subconscious mind, a more dominant will urged us to drink — at any cost, with no holds barred. We admit that sin played a part in our sickness, but as a result, rather than its cause.

We believe that turning one's will over to the care of God is vital for A.A. members. It is surely something to do with all sincerity, for recovery is a life and death affair for most of us. A matter in which only a decision born of sincerity and desperation will kill that deeply buried urge — to drink at any cost. Step 3 suggests the only way we know of diverting an alcoholic's will from drunkenness to sobriety.

It is not a Step of slavery but of freedom from self-centered willfulness. It gives us mastery of our will by sublimating its destructive energy with love, service and spiritual power. By this practice, we convert our creative forces within to constructive use and regulate to great extent, our circumstances without. Thus enlightened about our will and the inward thoughts which mold our destiny, we are ready to turn our will to drink at any cost over to the care of "God as we understand Him."

TURNING OUR LIVES OVER TO GOD

Leaving our "understanding of God" to be discussed under the third division of this Step, we now propose an investigation of the present circumstances of our lives. Having admitted that they are unmanageable, we would learn how to place them in God's care.

Step Three poses certain unpleasant issues which we have dodged for years. What has drinking done to our lives? Have we deteriorated spiritually because of drinking? What is an alcoholic's life?

For normal people, life is a vital thing — a series of happy experiences of mind and body, exciting them to acts of creative, useful service. It is a conscious, living state of growth and reproduction which brings them peace of mind and zest for further living. It has that animated quality which distinguishes between dead and living things.

Can we, by any stretch of imagination, establish our daily drinking experiences as normal? Were our lives like that? Hardly! They do not pass this simple test of normal living.

Some members would like to forget their unmanageable lives, but it is not a safe thing to do. A complete personality change is in order. We should remember this when we make a decision to turn our will and our lives over to the helpful guidance of a Higher Power.

Remember, also, that our lives were not what alcoholic rationalization made them out to be. They had very little in common with normal lives, with one exception: although spiritually emaciated, we were not really dead.

We often wished to die but could not. The longer we lived, the more we drank. The more we drank, the less we had to live for. The less we had to live for, the more we rationalized our reason for living. Such was the progressive nature of our alcoholic illness. Such is the nature of the life that alcohol exacted from us, the life which we now entrust to God's care.

Considering the fact that we are "powerless over alcohol" and that we can no longer endure our unmanageable lives, we are lucky, indeed, to find a simple means of rehabilitation in A.A. Our recovery starts when we admit our powerlessness and ask God for help.

Our egos, long pickled in alcohol, will never cease fighting this honest reality. It is advisable to face this circumstance with open minds — ready and willing to begin our recovery.

Why hide our heads in the sands of ignorance and rationalization? We need God's help. We must have it. Otherwise we cannot recover from our spiritual illness. Failing in that, we cannot recover at all.

There is a great difference between agreeing with Step 3 and in trying to live it. A dangerous difference for an alcoholic, for one is compliance — the other surrender. Alcoholics comply, but fight surrender.

The human mind knows when we are in earnest. It winks knowingly at compliance but willingly obeys complete surrender. Under surrender's powerful, regenerative urge, it properly deflates our super-charged egos and kills that hidden will to drink at any cost.

Summing up the good and bad characteristics of the lives we bring into A.A., we find them, just as described in Step 1, powerless over alcohol and unmanageable. Compulsive drinking has confused our thinking and made us physically, mentally and spiritually ill. These are the end results of our alcoholic living. Our plan in A.A. is to arrest them before they ruin us.

65

From this dark picture it might seem that the future held nothing for us, that our inherent capabilities for constructive living were dead. This would be true but for one fact. We all retain a source of untapped power which is to be found in our spiritual possibilities. Through them we attain life's greatest blessings. But unless we try to develop them, we will sink to life's lowest estate.

Some people rob themselves. Some are robbed by others. But no one can ever rob us of a happy, sober life if we will develop our spiritual power, as Step 3 recommends.

Having arrived at an honest understanding of the harmful, purposeless nature of our alcoholic lives, there should be no question about what we propose entrusting to God's care. This brings our discussion up to the last division of Step Three.

"GOD AS WE UNDERSTOOD HIM"

It may appear presumptuous to discuss a definite plan of understanding God and of having personal contact with Him, but since it is the ultimate result of Step Three there is no other choice. It seems fitting that one alcoholic should willingly explain his understanding of God to another. For who but another alcoholic would listen or hope to gain any help from it?

Understanding God is not beyond our power of reason and attainment. We begin to sense His help as soon as we make our decision and start living the 12 Steps. Personality changes in the lives of members who live the Steps are proof of this. Evidence is found in their happy, sober lives. We can vouch for these facts. It is the explanation of our daily contact with

God which defied description. It cannot be defined. We are not spiritually awakened by a single act but by many A.A. thoughts and acts which we perform each day.

It would be convenient if we could perform an outstanding accomplishment and immediately qualify as spiritual people. At this writing there seems to be no standard for attainment of this goal. Many alcoholics have tried it without success. Being alcoholics we still try. That seems to be the nature of our personalities—to look for shortcuts. But spiritual shortcuts are decidedly dangerous. They lead in one direction only — that is back toward the bottle and more drinking.

Step Three suggests that we try to attain a better understanding of moral values, that we show our willingness to learn God's will by discipline of our own will. This requires the practice of faith, humility and courage. We should cultivate these personality traits until, by their daily practice, we form new spiritual habits.

In reality, our future security is dependent upon our willingness to be reborn from lives of alcoholic deterioration to healthy, sober lives ruled by just motives and maintained by a regular spiritual contact with God.

The secret of successful recovery is surrender. Surrender of what? Surrender of false pride, spiritual prejudice and our other alcoholic weaknesses to a Higher Power for help.

We try to surrender as completely as possible, for members who are willing to settle for less than their best efforts often fail to recover. We know of no way to escape this reality. Our best interests are served when we do not attempt it.

It is inconsistent to refuse life and sobriety through the medium of the 12 Steps. Our program is not hard to follow. The 12 Steps are simple. A.A. life is simple. If daily practice of the 12 Steps opens the way to spiritual living, then our approach to an understanding of God becomes simple.

When ready, we will overcome our egotism and see the network of alcoholic delusions in which our thinking has become entrapped. To live we must end the reservations which jeopardize our recovery. We shall then stop speculating about God and try to utilize His help. Some alcoholics rise to positions of great understanding, service and power with this help. Others remain in helpless confusion without it.

Suppose that we are willing to

try to understand God's Will but are opposed by biased, prejudiced and agnostic views. How can we overcome them?

We will require a strong incentive to establish a "conscious contact with God." Alcoholics have this incentive. It is found in Steps One and Two. Life and sanity are the considerations. If God is the only one who can help us preserve them, it seems foolish to refuse such an available source of help.

We should be open-minded and try to get our spiritual understanding by living the 12 Steps. Unmanageable alcoholic lives are incentive enough to start us working out our own interpretation and understanding of a Higher Power. This is slow in the beginning, but we will gain in wisdom and grow in strength each day.

Without attempting to define

71

God, perhaps we can improve our understanding by considering the qualities which are attributed to Him. Then, as we acquire some of these qualities, our lives will be enriched, and spiritual progress will become easier.

What are these qualities? Do they result from 12 Step living? Yes, we think so. Here are a few of them.

Qualities we commonly associate with God, from which A.A. members gain benefit, are such things as: honesty — sincerity — good motives — moral courage — creative energy — intelligence — decency — reason — virtue — peace — composure — justice — fair dealings — hope — truth — conscience — faith — honor — open-mindedness — charity — mercy — compassion — humility — appreciation — tolerance — forgiveness — service and love.

There are many who believe that the last two attributes embrace all the rest.

We have yet to meet an alcoholic who is devoid of all these qualities. Nobody is completely bad, no matter how poor his reputation. Illness, remorse and despair often make us indifferent to life's moral values, but given the right inspiration we will accept them. There is some good in the worst of us. It may be fighting for life, but it is still there. In A.A., where there is life, there is hope for recovery.

What is this spark of good within us? Is it God waiting to be understood? How shall we locate and interpret it? With no evidence to the contrary, we feel justified in calling it our spiritual possibility. It could be a "Power greater than ourselves" located within our hearts and minds. What we call It is of no consequence.

73

The fact that we all have It, believe in It, and improve upon It is the only thing which matters.

Spiritual awakening in man is a natural response to universal law, a means by which he elevates himself to power above his physical limitations. This inherent possibility must be developed. It is not available on demand. Alcoholics can neither buy nor sell it. It is the reward of spiritual thought and endeavor. We earn it bit by bit. Its wage is faithful effort.

By faith we open the way to A.A. understanding. By love and service we kill prejudice and allow God to enter the dungeon walls of alcoholic thinking. He enters by the secret door of surrender when we are entirely ready to lose our drinking allergy and our mental obsession.

When this happens He gives us the key to contented sobriety. Step 3 is the key. It outlines a workable plan of action. We simply work it to the extent of our ability and pray that God will do the rest. To date He has not let us down.

Our knowledge of God will come as we lose ourselves in 12 Step living. As we develop our talent in this service, He gives us understanding of His Will for us. Part of it comes from the inspiration we receive as we surrender our will and lives to Him. The rest is a matter of prayer, meditation, faith and willing service.

Our mental attitude is important. Motivated by desire and willingness to recover from our illness, we develop spiritual strength and understanding. It comes slowly from simple daily acts such as admitting our wrongs, taking inventory of our character defects, becoming forgiving of others, practicing honesty, humility, tolerance, love, anonymity, making amends and "carrying the message" to other alcoholics.

Step 3 adds a third leg to our recovery stool. Its simple requirement is a final decision to surrender our will to drink to "God as we understand Him" and to gain our understanding of Him by living the 12 Steps. To do this we must learn a few facts about ourselves. It's time to pull up our stool to the inventory table and go to work.

STEP FOUR

"Made a searching and fearless moral inventory of ourselves."

In terms of A.A. progress our inventories are most essential. They are fully as important at this time as our decisions were in Step 3. We all know that decision without action serves no worthwhile purpose, and neither does A.A. without Step 4.

To admit our alcoholism, with all its hidden defects, is not enough. We have always suspected they were there but never went to the trouble of listing them before. This is also true of the sorrow and injury which our drinking habits have brought to others.

Step 4 actuates our decisions. It starts us listing the defective character traits which have separated us from God, making our lives unstable and ineffective. This inventory is needed for several reasons. First, to learn our character defects so we may correct them. Second, to prepare us for taking Step 5. Third, to visualize the amends we owe to those whom our drinking has injured.

If we aspire toward more than temporary A.A. benefits, it will be wise to make a thorough written inventory. We should not procrastinate, for anything which the alcoholic mind puts off indefinitely is likely to go undone.

We often meet people in our fellowship who are not taking the full A.A. treatment. But we never let that stop us from our own recovery efforts.

Suppose Joe Blurp may say,

"Nuts to the inventory. I never wrote one. I'm sober." Joe gives a misleading picture of his true A.A. status. He is sober all right but cocky and unhappy about it. Eventually he may get drunk or leave A.A. Quite often he does both. Must we follow in Joe's egotistical footsteps? No, not at all. If we wish to recover, we will safeguard our sobriety by writing our inventories. Like Joe, we have much to learn about dry drunkenness. Our inventories will disclose its symptoms.

The quickest way to physical drunkenness for A.A. members is via the mental binge. When sober, this is hard to realize, but it is true.

The following pages are devoted to eight of our most common character defects. They contribute largely to all mental drunkenness in A.A. They all belong in our inventories because of their harmful effect upon our lives.

RESENTMENT

Resentment is like a double-edged sword. It cuts two ways, injuring us more than it wounds another. Alcoholics know that it harms them more for it leads them back to drinking.

A.A. states that resentment is the "number one offender" among our members, that it puts more alcoholics in their graves than any other thing.

Its subtle action is cunningly contrived to deceive us regarding the danger of its use. Resentful members may be physically sober but very drunk mentally. (Spiritual illness.)

Resentment makes slaves of us all, binding us with mental chains to the thing we hate. We find our release in prayer. We cannot hate and pray for anything at the same time.

A.A.
DRY
DRUNK

RESENTMENT

(A. A. Rotgut)

Distilled from Stinking Thinking and all the other alcoholic Character Defects.

Repeated snorts from this bottle are guaranteed to maintain mental and spiritual illness.

This drink obstructs all effort to turn your will and life over to the care of God.

If you are trying to escape humility—honesty—A.A. service and contented sobriety. drink freely.

Alcoholics have great success falling off the program and getting drunk with this drink.

DISHONESTY

Our founders placed the label of failure upon this bottle from which we have all imbibed so freely. They state that contented sobriety and dishonesty are incompatible. This is not because A.A. decrees it but because an alcoholic reacts that way.

The cause for this reaction is given in detail on page 70 in the original edition of *Alcoholics Anonymous* — on page 58 in the second edition. Study the chapter "How It Works" to learn why those who are dishonest with themselves cannot be honest with others and why being dishonest with ourselves starts us drinking again.

Dishonesty breeds fear, kills peace of mind, separates us from God, frustrates A.A. effort and makes us drink.

A.A.
DRY
DRUNK

DISHONESTY

(Double-crosser's Highball)

A special distillation from the pure essence of alcoholic inconsistency.

A favorite drink for male or female use where Fraud—Larceny—Chiseling—Chicanery—Drunkenness and Fear are the chief objectives.

Heavy doses of this drink will keep you at a disadvantage in A.A. — at home and among strangers.

You can depend upon dishonesty for miserable doghouse experiences.

You can't fail to fail in A.A. and to miss contented sobriety from repeated slugs out of this bottle.

CRITICISM

There is nothing for an alcoholic to be critical about in A.A. if he is there for the right purpose.

Members should look upon themselves as sick people and regard the A.A. program as a means of self-preservation, not something to be critical about.

In reality, A.A. becomes our school and hospital. Sponsors guide us, but we must develop our own strength by study and practice of the 12 Steps.

We fill the unique role of patient, intern, nurse and doctor, treating our illness under the care of "God as we understand Him."

A.A. efforts would prove fruitless if the world assumed a critical attitude toward our recovery. Let us keep this in mind when we become critical.

**A.A.
DRY
DRUNK**

CRITICISM

(Home-brewed Dissension)

This mental intoxicant is fomented from selected defects of the alcoholic personality.

It inoculates our minds with Rumors — Gossip — Fault-finding — Intolerance — Jealousy — Rebellion and Resentment. It spreads unwarranted suspicion. It kills A.A. unity.

Criticism is highly intoxicating. A choice drink for those still in the "driver's seat." The drink with the perpetual hangover.

Nothing threatens our sobriety or the group's safety any more than this cockeyed drink.

SELF-PITY

Pity is a feeling for the suffering of others. Self-pity is a gross misuse of this worthy feeling. It is an extreme form of self-centeredness which retards our spiritual growth. There are many reasons for self-pity and they are all bad.

Members who are daily addicts to this insidious mental poison lead unhappy lives and stand little chance for success in A.A. or elsewhere. To be filled with commiseration, compassion and sympathy for ourselves is an inferior feeling born of emotional instability. It stifles A.A. growth.

Self-pity is the brother of resentment. It is childish rebellion against God, people and circumstances. Appreciation is the antidote for its poison.

A.A.
DRY
DRUNK

SELF-PITY

(The Crying Jag of A. A.)

Don't underrate this mild mental beverage. It is slow acting, but it carries a knockout wallop.

Self-pity — the magic drink — helps you make mountains out of mole hills. Stay tight on this stuff, and you will become an A.A. weakling.

It magnifies your problems. It absorbs you with calamity's details until you cannot see the helpful opportunities about you.

Self-pity is rebellion in disguise — a rebellion against circumstances and against God's Will. Kill it with appreciation and faith.

INTOLERANCE

Tolerance, like a spiritual lubricant, reduces friction and keeps A.A. running smoothly on its bearings of humility and service. The 12 Steps are built upon tolerance. Without it there could be no A.A.

The disposition to tolerate beliefs and practices differing from our own is an important part of the personality change which the 12 Steps help us to develop. It is a good sign of emotional maturity in a member.

Intolerance is the opposite. It is that part of the alcoholic personality which we attempt to change. By checking this character defect daily we can determine just what sort of progress we are making. The written inventory of Step 4 is a good place to begin.

A.A.
DRY
DRUNK

INTOLERANCE

(Unadulterated Sourpuss Juice)

Intolerance, the fusel oil of mental drunkenness, quickly louses up your chances of recovery in A.A. It checks 12 Step enthusiasm.

It breeds spiritual illness. It never fails to give you that "to hell with everybody but me" feeling.

This drink is unsurpassed for blocking the freedom and happiness of family, friends and associates.

Nothing equals it for slips. If you want to be drunk — unhappy — unpopular and unattached to A.A., try intolerance. You may depend upon it for these results.

JEALOUSY

Jealousy can become a combination of every emotion, impulse and feeling. Each emotion has its good and bad characteristics, but not jealousy. It is made up of all their bad features.

Jealous members cannot live normal lives in A.A. They are motivated by fear, mistrust and resentment. In this mood we have no peace of mind. We lack faith in A.A. We do not trust God or our fellow members.

We aspire for offices we do not get and keep our groups in an uproar because of our strange obsession. Our envy exacts the exclusive devotion of others. It does not tolerate rivalry. Jealousy and criticism have broken up a lot of A.A. groups. We had better not overlook them in our inventory.

**A.A.
DRY
DRUNK**

JEALOUSY

(Dynamite Cocktail)

A strong blend of all the elements of mental drunkenness from the vats of fear and envy.

Contents: Fear — Anger — Resentment — Self-Pity — Dishonesty — Revenge — Intolerance and Hatred.

Daily use of this emotional monstrosity will prey upon the alcoholic mind until like a malignant cancer it injures or destroys it.

Jealousy of a person's affection — his standing, talents, possessions — shows a dangerous mental condition for any A.A. member.

ANGER

Anger is a strong emotion of displeasure which excites us to acts of antagonism, fury, rage and violence.

It is a human impulse loaded with mental and physical energy. But, since we have to live with it, we must learn how to divert it to constructive use. Most of the time we must kill it entirely; otherwise it may kill us.

Anger, in a broad sense, indicates a decided loss of self-control. Fury and wrath imply an overmastering passion verging on madness with an intent of revenge and punishment.

The 12 Steps are a spiritual way of life which directly opposes anger in all its phases. They are a means by which we learn to control its harmful influence. We inventory our anger.

A.A.
DRY
DRUNK

ANGER

(TNT Special)

A lethal concoction brewed from the knockout drops of straight mental poison. A choice drink for those who wish to play God.

A specific emotion aimed toward injury to others. Its end is to kill or destroy. Primitive man used it as a means of survival. A.A. suggests no instance where it benefits our members. On the contrary, we are warned to avoid it.

Anger opposes all 12 Step principles. It overrides reason. It insulates us from God and the spiritual help necessary for our recovery.

FEAR

Fear is a painful emotion marked by alarm, terror and anxiety. Its forces are well known to both the alcoholic and his family.

The family fears for the welfare of the alcoholic and for its own security. The alcoholic fears his own inadequacy to live normally because of his compulsive drinking.

Fear is a destructive energy which we have long used against ourselves. It belongs in our inventories as its use has been mostly negative. We find that our fears are closely associated with conscious guilt which undoubtedly stems from compulsive drinking.

Fear has survival values when used correctly. *The Little Red Book*, pages 69 to 75, covers fear in more detail.

A.A.
DRY
DRUNK

FEAR

(A. A. Jitters)

180 Proof — Effective — Quick Acting — Alarming — Frustrating — Terrifying — Paralyzing — Deadly.

Fear induces the energy to flee or duck reality. Drunk on this mental poison we placed distorted faith in ideas of harm to our health — lives — families — reputation — social standing — finance — anonymity — and sobriety.

Fear is contrary to our 12 Step philosophy. Its antidote is faith. Faith in the A.A. program to help us recover our health. Faith in God's power to perform the miracle of contented sobriety in our lives.

FIRST DAILY REMINDER

Let's be honest today. Let's face facts. Alcohol is a beverage for most people but is a drug for alcoholics. Our uncontrolled use of this narcotic has made us sick in body, mind and spirit. We are quite powerless over it. It threatens our lives and sanity.

DAILY INVENTORY

How alcoholic are we? Do we drink sanely? Are we all through fighting booze? Have we really hit bottom? Will we accept A.A.?

SUGGESTED MEDITATION

As sick alcoholics, we should join A.A. As members, we should recall daily that we are arresting an incurable illness. That we are sick — not plain crazy. Our uncontrolled drinking has placed us in a very bad spot. To take it or leave it alone — that is the question. Drinking alcoholics can do neither — that is our problem. To live sanely, we must leave it alone — that is a fact. Without A.A. this is impossible. A.A. is the best solution to our drinking problem.

SPIRITUAL CONTACT

Our Father, give us an understanding of our illness. Strengthen our efforts to overcome it. Lead us in the paths of contented sobriety.

DAILY PHYSICAL AUDIT

A.A. is made up of persons who are attempting to compensate for a lifetime of mistakes. That is the premise upon which our recovery program is based. Through study and honest endeavor, we arrest our mental and spiritual malady, yet pass lightly over our physical illness. The baffling part of alcoholism is our disregard for health. We depend too much upon curing disease when we should be building up healthy bodies to prevent it.

SECOND DAILY REMINDER

Sick — Desperate — Helpless, we called upon A.A. Help came. Not later, but that very day. That is how A.A. works, day by day. With yesterday as "water over the dam" our tomorrow can become a happy, sober one — if we willingly live the A.A. program today.

DAILY INVENTORY

Does false pride keep us from admitting our alcoholism? Shall we clean yesterday's slate? Shall we start a new life in A.A. today?

SUGGESTED MEDITATION

The sad failures which plague our lives today are not results of chance. They did not occur overnight. We earned them. They are the payoff for a thousand drunken yesterdays. But — they are not the end. We can rebuild new, happy, sober lives upon their costly ruins.

Twenty-four hour drinking has made us ill. Twenty-four hour A.A. living will make us well. Our drinking time has about run out. Perhaps we should start living the A.A. program today.

SPIRITUAL CONTACT

Our Father, direct our thinking. Teach us to make right decisions. Start us rebuilding our unstable lives day by day. Grant us the power to do this.

DAILY PHYSICAL AUDIT

Years of hard drinking have robbed us of body building nutrition, minerals and needed vitamins. It will take time to replace them. A.A. cannot do this. We must design our physical recovery around a systematic daily intake of nutritious, health building foods and regular periods of relaxation. Health is essential to our recovery — we should consider it each day.

THIRD DAILY REMINDER

Before A.A., alcoholics were faced with lives of untold suffering and despair. An awesome future compared with ours — for we may choose between drinking and contented sobriety. Why we deserve the miracle of A.A. is a question too baffling for us to answer but most worthy of thought and appreciation.

DAILY INVENTORY

Is A.A. an inspired program? Are we deserving of it? Do we appreciate its health and life giving opportunities? Are we willing to work them?

SUGGESTED MEDITATION

Could God in His dealing with A.A. have said, "Show Me your willingness to live in sobriety and I will perform the miracle of contented sobriety in your lives. I will give you the book Alcoholics Anonymous. *In it are the answers to all your alcoholic problems. You shall have a little wisdom and a little strength, and I will leave the door to your recovery ajar. I believe in you. Do not let Me down!"*

SPIRITUAL CONTACT

Our Father, we realize that our recovery from alcoholism depends upon our physical and spiritual conditions. Help us to improve them daily.

DAILY PHYSICAL AUDIT

The Big Book tells us to remember that compulsive drinking has damaged us physically—that our health is usually bad upon entering A.A. It recommends "hospitalization for the alcoholic who is very jittery or befogged," to clear his mind so that he may comprehend the recovery program which A.A. offers him. Sponsors should endeavor to follow this policy wherever possible.

FOURTH DAILY REMINDER

Hopefully, yet doubtfully, we came to our first A.A. meeting. There we found understanding and sympathy but gained no peace of mind. Still riding in the driver's seat, we were full of anxiety over the future. We saw A.A. working for others, but our case seemed hopeless. How could it work for us?

DAILY INVENTORY

Can loneliness and self-pity prevent A.A. progress? How can we overcome them? Does anxiety indicate lack of faith? Will A.A. work for us?

SUGGESTED MEDITATION

Loneliness gives us a strong incentive to drink. A.A. kills it with friendship. It's up to us to cultivate A.A. friends. Anxiety blocks 12 Step living. It indicates a lack of faith in God and is a form of fear.

We need moral courage to live A.A. — to vacate the driver's seat and to kill self-pity and fear. It also takes courage to face another drunk. A.A. works if we choose the right kind of courage.

SPIRITUAL CONTACT

Our Father, we pray for faith and spiritual courage to face our problems. Grant us wisdom to know our weakness and strength to rebuild our lives.

DAILY PHYSICAL AUDIT

Alcoholics suffer from dietary disturbances because they have received about one-third of their calories from alcohol which contains no proteins, vitamins or minerals. Rehabilitative life in A.A. affords us an opportunity to progressively replenish this deficiency with a daily, balanced diet adequate for our physical needs and well-being.

103

FIFTH DAILY REMINDER

Our *A.A.* book states that we either kill self-centeredness or that it will kill us; that we are "extreme examples of self-will run riot" — would-be big shots, unable to run our own lives. This seems unbelievable and hard to admit yet we cannot recover until we do admit and fully believe it.

DAILY INVENTORY

How about self-centeredness? Will it ruin us? Do we live unstable lives? Is today the time to stop this "I" complex and start living in terms of "We"?

SUGGESTED MEDITATION

Self-centeredness opposes every spiritual principle. Alcoholics have always met defeat by defying these principles. By playing God, by drinking and bragging, "I did this—I did that—if it hadn't been for me," we rationalized in alcoholic bunk. We mistook insanity and slavery

*for power and freedom. A.A. will help us
to overcome this slavery. Our first step
toward freedom, however, lies in freedom
from self.*

SPIRITUAL CONTACT

Our Father, forgive us our self-centeredness and the harm it has caused others. We pray for knowledge of Thy will for us. Thy will be done.

DAILY PHYSICAL AUDIT

Members often arrive in A.A. on the verge of delirium and physical exhaustion. They need hospitalization, rest, medical care and physical rebuilding by intravenous and normal feeding.

We should not forget that a narcotic as powerful as alcohol has damaged our bodies. Nature needs our help and cooperation to overcome this damage. We slow up our recovery when we ignore this fact.

SEVENTH DAILY REMINDER

We cannot overemphasize the importance of admitting "our powerlessness over alcohol" or that "our lives had become unmanageable" because of our addiction to it. Lasting sobriety demands this admission. We should attribute our illness to alcoholism (a disease), rather than to lack of will power.

DAILY INVENTORY

Why must we admit our alcoholism? Is this just an alibi for drinking? If we must stay sober in A.A., why can't we do so through willpower?

SUGGESTED MEDITATION

A.A. starts working the moment we admit our alcoholism and ask for help to treat it. Admitting our need for help energizes the powerful forces of honesty and humility within us. They are the rudi-

ments of recovery. We need not alibi.
Alcoholism is a disease which sickens our
bodies and minds. We should ask God to
heal our spiritual illness. We treat our
bodies with medical care—not with will
power.

SPIRITUAL CONTACT

Our Father, we admit our alcoholism. Help us to recover from it. We wish to co-operate. Teach us how to rebuild our lives — physically and spiritually.

DAILY PHYSICAL AUDIT

Probably all A.A. members should be examined by a competent doctor to determine their liver conditions. Many have fatty livers and some have mild cirrhosis of the liver. The majority are free from this disease. We should know about our condition, however, and receive medical care when it is needed. Caught early enough, these diseases can be successfully treated.

109

EIGHTH DAILY REMINDER

Surely, there is insanity in alcoholism — not only in that first drink but in the endless drunks which followed. Having failed to stop drinking under our own power, we have reached the end of human resources. A.A. suggests that we surrender our insane behavior to the care of a Higher Power.

DAILY INVENTORY

Is there mental illness in our alcoholism? Are we helpless against it? How can we overcome it? Must our help come from a Higher Power?

SUGGESTED MEDITATION

As we weigh the insanity of alcoholism, we must face the fact that no matter how honest our resolve or how sane our plan—we always managed to get plastered. Few persons equaled us in stupidity or self-deception. We alibied our mis-

takes but refused to profit from them. Filled with liquor and distorted ideas, we lacked the sanity of self-preservation which only God can give to a drinking alcoholic.

SPIRITUAL CONTACT

Our Father, make us realize the insanity of our drinking behavior. Give us faith in Your Power to restore in us the instinct of self-preservation.

DAILY PHYSICAL AUDIT

A.A. tells us that we are sick in body and mind, saying, "in our belief . . . any picture which leaves out this physical factor is incomplete." Health aids sobriety. Let's not neglect it. Sensible precaution may save us the unhappy experience of a relapse. It may uncover the presence of disease in time for preventive care.

NINTH DAILY REMINDER

Reservation, doubt and fear assail the minds of newcomers and impede their recovery in A.A. Salesmen doubt their ability to sell without the aid of alcohol. Some fear that their identity will be disclosed. Others wonder how to avoid bars and drinking friends or what alibi to offer for their sobriety.

DAILY INVENTORY

Can we hold reservations and live the 12 Steps? Is fear a sign of future failure? Do we avoid drinking friends? How does A.A. answer these questions?

SUGGESTED MEDITATION

The book Alcoholics Anonymous *holds the answers to all of our recovery problems. From it we learn that distrust and fear are dangerous mental attitudes for alcoholics to hold. It suggests that our security and sobriety will come from faith in God and practice of the 12 Steps. It explains our future conduct with drinking friends and the reason we give them for our abstinence. See your Big Book.*

SPIRITUAL CONTACT

Our Father, replace our reservations and fear with faith, courage and A.A. understanding. Inspire us with an honest desire to succeed in A.A.

DAILY PHYSICAL AUDIT

After varying periods of sobriety we often complain of physical fatigue, vague pain, arthritis, gastric disturbances and insomnia. We attribute them to the sober lives we are leading and reach for a box of pills or some patented elixir. There are better antidotes for health. Perhaps we should lower our daily cigarette and coffee consumptions, stop living on coffee and dessert and try sleeping eight hours every night.

113

TENTH DAILY REMINDER

A "water over the dam" policy of dealing with our past drinking behavior is the only basis upon which we can rehabilitate ourselves. By living A.A. we learn how our drinking has affected the lives of others. We feel remorseful, but that does not repay the injury done. A.A. suggests that we amend it.

DAILY INVENTORY

Are we trying to rehabilitate our lives? Have we a list of the people whom we have harmed? Are we willing to make proper amends to them?

SUGGESTED MEDITATION

Yes, we are trying to rebuild our lives to conform with 12 Step principles and to live in contented sobriety, but not at the expense of others. Live and let live— that is our motto. The water over the dam is forgotten, but not the injury done. We need forgiveness to recover from our illness. To accept it without return defies

114

all spiritual law and threatens our sobriety. Amends are good for our conscience.

SPIRITUAL CONTACT

Our Father, forgive us the harm we have done to others. May we become forgiving. Fortify our minds with willingness to make proper amends.

DAILY PHYSICAL AUDIT

From medical science we learn that the main causes of death are related to our blood and its circulation. Heart trouble ranks high under this category. Alcoholics are not exceptions to the rule. Many members die needlessly because they ignore the warning symptoms of heart trouble and treat it too late. Pain and numbness in the arms, fatigue, labored breathing after mild exercise, heartburn and water in the tissues are symptoms our doctors should diagnose.

ELEVENTH DAILY REMINDER

We have often wished for help and peace of mind during the throes of our hangovers. We have prayed for help but seldom prayed for permanent sobriety. We wanted alcohol's narcotic effects without its penalties. But our prayers always failed. Some barrier seemed to separate us from contented sobriety.

DAILY INVENTORY

What was this barrier? Were we unconsciously praying for some form of controlled drinking? Is an inventory in order? Must we list our defects?

SUGGESTED MEDITATION

A.A. forces no "musts" upon us any-more than drinking friends would force a drink down our throats. Alcoholics do as they please, either in or outside of A.A.— that's why we are here. "Musts" are voluntary. Wise members, recalling the torture of their drinking days, list their character defects. Those awful hangovers were not just nightmares. They can recur. An honest inventory might prevent them.

SPIRITUAL CONTACT

Our Father, keep us open-minded and ready to earn the greatest help possible from living the 12 Steps. Help us to write an honest inventory.

DAILY PHYSICAL AUDIT

Thousands of people who have heart trouble live long and happy lives by calmly admitting their illness and cooperating with their doctors in treating it. The great hope for prolonged life among those affected with heart disease is to live within the functional limits of the weakened organ. The chief prescription is rest. Things to avoid are fatigue, overeating, infection, obesity and emotional upsets.

117

TWELFTH DAILY REMINDER

"Made a decision." How easy it is to partly fulfill each of the 12 Steps. But how hard to decide that we are sick enough to "turn our will and our lives over to the care of God." How hard to seek our understanding of God's Will. How easy it is to mistake half-hearted lip service for decision and surrender.

DAILY INVENTORY

Are we in A.A. for the ride? Have we decided that we need God's help to live soberly? Are we sincere about it or are we just giving lip service?

SUGGESTED MEDITATION

There is no middle of the road course for a drinking alcoholic—he is either wet or dry. A.A. represents a similar case in the 12 Steps vs. John Barleycorn. Since we cannot drink and live, our choice will be A.A. With our lives at stake, we can ill afford to depend upon lip service for pro-

tection. Recovery from alcoholism is a serious matter for us. We need both the 12 Steps and God's help to recover.

SPIRITUAL CONTACT

Our Father, deliver us this day from defiance, doubt and indecision. Teach us the value of obedience. Stabilize our thinking according to our need.

DAILY PHYSICAL AUDIT

Man is a creature of many habits. Alcoholics have formed bad eating and drinking habits which are not conducive to good health. Some of us become overweight from taking more food than our bodies can assimilate. This throws an extra burden on the heart which increases our blood pressure and shortens our lives. We should watch our diet to guard against coronary disease, apoplexy and other ills associated with overweight.

119

THIRTEENTH DAILY REMINDER

The virtues of anonymity are many and far reaching for our older members. For the newcomer anonymity has a special meaning. Its strong appeal is secrecy. A hideout in which to recover without publicity or blame. Anonymity is our privilege to use but also our obligation to protect.

DAILY INVENTORY

Have we realized the true value of anonymity? What are some of its spiritual values? Is it our obligation to protect the identity of other members?

SUGGESTED MEDITATION

Anonymity is vital to an A.A. group. Helping another person anonymously is a spiritual act—the very lifeblood of A.A. There should be no breach of anonymity. Secrecy is a part of alcoholic thinking. We tried to conceal our drink-

*ing and told lies about hangovers. No-
body could believe them. Anonymity did
not work for drinking, but it does work
for our recovery. It lets us work with
others, also.*

SPIRITUAL CONTACT

Our Father, we thank You for
A.A. Help us to live its program, to
understand its principles and to
learn the spiritual values of anonymity.

DAILY PHYSICAL AUDIT

There is nothing anonymous
about a member's poor physical
health. It can be detected by his
fuzzy thinking, his lack of enthusiasm, the sweaty palms of his hands
and his inaptitude toward normal
daily recovery. Poor physical health
causes nervousness and irritability
at meetings. It leads to intolerant
and resentful thinking. It can get us
drunk. Members are not blamed for
being ill, but they owe it to themselves to get well.

FOURTEENTH DAILY REMINDER

Many of us have stumbled over the term *spiritual awakening*. By confusing A.A. with organized religion, we have encountered trouble with the spiritual angle. By trying to define God and to interpret A.A. according to religious creeds, we have experienced frustration and ineffectual A.A. living.

DAILY INVENTORY

Are the objectives of A.A. and organized religion the same? Is our objective to save souls? Are there signs which identify a spiritual awakening?

SUGGESTED MEDITATION

A.A. offers a 24-hour program borrowed from medicine, religion and psychology by which we arrest alcoholism, an incurable illness. It utilizes physical, mental and spiritual help to maintain

24-hour periods of contented sobriety. It suggests a daily contact with God as we understand Him. A.A. is not a religion. We see in honesty, sobriety, forgiveness, amends and love signs of a spiritual awakening.

SPIRITUAL CONTACT

Our Father, we recognize the latent spiritual power within us and ask Your help to develop it. Awaken us to our spiritual possibilities.

DAILY PHYSICAL AUDIT

There are no written tests to pass in A.A. How we recover is a matter of our own choice. We may either sink or swim. But swimming requires good physical health. So does satisfactory recovery from alcoholism. We ought to recognize this fact and live to improve the quality of our health and thus enjoy life to its full capacity. A.A. members are most effective when in good physical condition.

123

FIFTEENTH DAILY REMINDER

At times our vitality is low. Being restless and jittery, we have an urge to drink. Irritable, unhappy and self-centered, we work back into our favorite spot — the driver's seat. Resentment, worry and intolerance cloud our thinking. It is hard to pray. We miss meetings and neglect helping others.

DAILY INVENTORY

How do we account for our run-down and jittery feelings? Why these urges to drink? Why is it so hard to pray? What can we do about it?

SUGGESTED MEDITATION

A run-down physical condition makes an alcoholic jittery and creates an urge to drink. Overwork, lack of rest and wrong diet foster resentful attitudes of self-pity and intolerance. Such attitudes insulate us from God. They kill our peace of mind and end in drunkeness. We must recognize these symptoms and remove their causes. To eat, work, rest, play and pray intelligently helps to attain this end.

SPIRITUAL CONTACT

Our Father, teach us the meaning of "first things first." Endow us with sufficient common sense to maintain a healthy physical body.

DAILY PHYSICAL AUDIT

The road to recovery for our members is beset with pitfalls, some of which are physical. Alcoholism often depletes our nervous energy. Members who continue to overtax their nervous systems are courting trouble. Our minds cannot function apart from our bodies — nor can they function soundly in sick bodies. Obviously, it is to our best interest to rebuild physically.

SIXTEENTH DAILY REMINDER

Remember the old saying, "A chain is no stronger than its weakest link"? Alcoholism is the weak link in our chain of life and most confusing, too, for it embraces three weak links in one. They are the physical, mental and spiritual illness of alcoholism from which A.A. offers the best chance of recovery.

DAILY INVENTORY

Good? Better? Best? Plain sobriety or contented sobriety? Which shall it be? Shall we kill or improve our A.A. opportunities?

SUGGESTED MEDITATION

We joined A.A. to end the insanity of alcoholism and to live happy, sober lives. We admitted our illness and agreed to get well—not to get half well. Lack of self-preservation in A.A. seems like a new sort of insanity. Having made fair progress with our physical and mental health,

126

we should not refuse to grow up emotionally and spiritually. Recognizing this fact we should work for greater A.A. maturity.

SPIRITUAL CONTACT

Our Father, keep us aware of the fatal nature of our illness and the insanity of alcoholism. Help us mend the weak links in our personality chain.

DAILY PHYSICAL AUDIT

Budget your energy. Plan your activities for the day. Avoid emotional excitement. Set up daily periods for relaxation. Remember that your recovery should be physical as well as mental and spiritual. Physical fitness aids mental and spiritual recovery. We need to conserve our energy by heeding the feelings of fatigue which signal that our activities have become excessive. The result is a saving in energy which makes for better health.

SEVENTEENTH DAILY REMINDER

An old member got drunk but stopped drinking before any serious trouble developed. His group was none the wiser so he never told them of his relapse. He rationalized it as a minor slip and brazenly resumed old relations with his group. Uncertainty and fear dominated his progress, causing future relapses.

DAILY INVENTORY

How serious is a relapse? Should he have confided with the members of his group? What made him drink? Does A.A. forgive the slipper?

SUGGESTED MEDITATION

All slips are serious—some are fatal. Those called minor are unfinished drunks. They will be completed later. Dishonesty in some form is the basis of a slip. This member should have con-

fessed to his group. As A.A. patients, our minds are still alcoholic. We think in terms of drinking if we cannot be honest with ourselves. Slippers are ill. A.A. cannot forgive an illness, but it can help sick members to get well.

SPIRITUAL CONTACT

Our Father, we pray for help to become strictly honest with You and with ourselves. Free us from fear, dishonesty and relapses.

DAILY PHYSICAL AUDIT

Is there an aspect of dishonesty in abusing the body which God has entrusted to our care? Are we honest with Him, ourselves, our group, and the alcoholic "who still suffers" if from tension, overwork and physical neglect we are too ill or exhausted to contribute to the welfare of our group, or "carry the message" to the alcoholic who needs our help? Think it over. Perhaps this obligation has not occurred to you.

129

EIGHTEENTH DAILY REMINDER

Vindictiveness is a stumbling block to recovery for many members. They go to meetings and talk the program but reserve the right to suspect and hate — also the privilege of revenge. They are the advocates of justified resentments. They miss contented sobriety and wonder why A.A. fails to work for them.

DAILY INVENTORY

Why is revenge so disturbing to an alcoholic's peace of mind? Is resentment justified? Do hatred and revenge bar our chances for contented sobriety?

SUGGESTED MEDITATION

Our revengeful attitudes are indicative of reservations to the A.A. program. They oppose a great fundamental principle which requires us to forgive before we can be forgiven. Resentment and vindictiveness are forms of mental drunkenness which A.A. never justifies. Revengeful alcoholics are off their 12 Step base. Prayer puts them back on again. We should try praying for those we hate. It pays well.

SPIRITUAL CONTACT

Our Father, alert us to the future drunkenness which lies in attitudes of hatred and revenge. Help us to overcome them by praying for those we hate.

DAILY PHYSICAL AUDIT

How often do we meditate upon the value of a healthy body to help arrest our alcoholism? Not enough, to be sure. What a shame to wait until some illness disables us before we realize the positive necessity of good health to our recovery. We need observe only a few simple rules to keep well. Systematic living habits which give us adequate exercise, fresh air, sunlight, food and rest are essential to a healthy body.

NINETEENTH DAILY REMINDER

A sincere group of newcomers, discussing the various merits of the A.A. program, agreed that without surrender an alcoholic could not recover from his illness. There was one dissenter who flatly condemned surrender as a negative mental attitude, branding it, "the cowardly act of a defeatist."

DAILY INVENTORY

Who was right? Are we defeatists? Is surrender so vital to our recovery? What is it that we surrender? How do we go about it?

SUGGESTED MEDITATION

Foolhardy describes the behavior of a diabetic who, refusing insulin, gorges himself with sugar. Insane describes the behavior of an alcoholic who will not admit his illness and keeps on drinking. We do not ignore broken bones. We have them set. Alcoholism is like a broken bone for us. Asking God to set this alcoholic fracture is a mark of intelligence. Surrender, to be sure, but only to a constructive power.

SPIRITUAL CONTACT

Our Father, save us from intellectual folly. Elevate us above the hairsplitting of words. Show us the logic of surrendering our alcoholism to You.

DAILY PHYSICAL AUDIT

We cannot choose the body we start life with, but we are responsible for its daily care. There are members who do not seem to understand that God does not help us physically when we refuse to help ourselves. They vainly pray for help instead of calling upon a surgeon to remove an infected appendix, tooth or tonsil. We should not delay taking our health problems to capable doctors with whom God has so abundantly supplied us.

133

TWENTIETH DAILY REMINDER

The shortest route to a relapse in A.A. is to sober up without acquiring honesty, humility and a conscious contact with God. A good way to prevent this is suggested by Step 5. From it we derive many essentials of recovery, such as: humility, freedom from fear, honesty and spiritual inspiration.

DAILY INVENTORY

Are we among those who have delayed taking Step Five? Is there a legitimate reason for holding off any longer? Why not arrange to take Step Five now?

SUGGESTED MEDITATION

Members frequently take their sobriety too much for granted. They forget that alcoholism is an incurable disease. They go to A.A. meetings, admit their weak spots and mouth a few A.A. truths, yet cling tenaciously to some of their worst character defects. Their record of lip service is excellent, but their A.A. service is poor. Taking Step Five will uncover these facts. It keeps us humble and willing to serve.

SPIRITUAL CONTACT

Our Father, free us from the doldrums of A.A. procrastination. Fill us with 12 Step enthusiasm. Give us the moral courage to take Step Five.

DAILY PHYSICAL AUDIT

Everyone has blood pressure. Some have it high. Some have it low. Some have it normal. High blood pressure damages the blood vessels and is the most common cause of heart disease for members. Its causes are unknown, but it is often associated with kidney disease, with functional disturbance of the nervous system, the endocrine glands and with overweight. We should watch our blood pressure closely and keep it within our normal range.

135

TWENTY-FIRST DAILY REMINDER

After a few months of unhappy sobriety, a disgruntled A.A. member left his group and resumed drinking. He openly opposed certain spiritual parts of our program, labeling them "opium for the masses" and vowed that A.A. could not run his life. He won his point but by drinking lost his job, wife and home.

DAILY INVENTORY

Could he have been rebelling against the provisions of Steps Six and Seven? With regard to self-discipline, what are the functions of these steps?

SUGGESTED MEDITATION

The sign of outward depression in an alcoholic is only the shadow of the real oppression within. He is a very sick person ruled by a strong obsession which says, "I want to be free. I want to think and to drink as I please. I refuse to part with my character flaws — A.A. or no A.A." Such freedom only adds to our alcoholic bondage. Such spiritual rebellion is mental drunkeness—another slavery for us.

SPIRITUAL CONTACT

Our Father, illuminate our defects of character. Help us to enforce self-discipline. Grant us a willing desire to fully accept Steps 6 and 7.

DAILY PHYSICAL AUDIT

Modern medicine emphasizes diet as a powerful factor of healthful living. It claims we eat too much bread, fats and sugar at the expense of proteins, carbohydrates, mineral salts and vitamins which support body growth and repair. Chemical reaction in the alcoholic's body is impaired by lack of proper food. Our diet should be well balanced and fortified with ample vegetables, fruits and meat.

TWENTY-SECOND DAILY REMINDER

Having gained sobriety from living the A.A. program, it is easy to become overconfident about our future security. We often mistake recovery for cure and get off the A.A. beam. Satisfied with our progress and impressed by our evident maturity we become complacent and are ready to graduate from A.A.

DAILY INVENTORY

What is complacency? Is it a danger signal? Do we ever reach full maturity in A.A.? Are there specific graduation qualifications? Name them.

SUGGESTED MEDITATION

The Big Book gives the answers for all of our drinking problems. It also gives an A.A. graduation test on page 42 in the old book, or page 31 in the second edition. "If anyone, who is showing inability to control his drinking, can do the right-about-face and drink like a gentleman, our hats are off to him." Complacency *(self-satisfaction) is not for us. Our goal is serenity—the reward for daily A.A. living.*

SPIRITUAL CONTACT

Our Father, we pray that we may realize our need for daily A.A. living. Manifest the dangers of complacency to us. Teach us the meaning of serenity.

DAILY PHYSICAL AUDIT

Alcoholics are physically ill from toxic poisoning acquired by substituting alcohol for food and rest. We are impatient people who want to get well fast. It is not uncommon for newcomers to resort to the self-administration of drugs and antibiotics. This is a dangerous practice from which we suffer ill effects. Sedation is most harmful because it is habit forming. A.A. is ineffective for the willful users of self-administered drugs.

TWENTY-THIRD DAILY REMINDER

The keys to A.A. success and service are found in the last eight words of Step 12, "to practice these principles in all our affairs." It takes a lot of constructive thought, effort and courage to arrest our alcoholism — not the physical kind, but the moral courage to be honest with ourselves and live A.A.

DAILY INVENTORY

Is there more to Step 12 than just "carrying the message"? What about "a spiritual awakening"? What is meant by "these principles"?

SUGGESTED MEDITATION

"These principles" cover all of the 12 Steps. "Carrying the message" to alcoholics is vital, indeed, but it is only a part of practicing "these principles in all our affairs." Without their practice there could be no recovery. Without it we

would have no examples of contented sobriety—no message to carry—no sponsorship—no A.A. Let us never forget the significance of the last eight words of Step 12.

SPIRITUAL CONTACT

Our Father, awaken us spiritually. Allow us to "carry the message" to alcoholics. Help us to stay sober and to live the 12 Steps 24 hours a day.

DAILY PHYSICAL AUDIT

Medical science has long been interested in the relation of blood sugar to the physical condition of the alcoholic and his lack of craving after eating.

Experience teaches us that compulsion to drink usually occurred when our stomachs were empty and our blood sugar low. We should remember this in A.A. and always try to maintain an adequate level of nutrition for defense against that first drink.

141

TWENTY-FOURTH DAILY REMINDER

An A.A. member with several years of sobriety and a record of active service moved to another city and attached himself to the local group. Working upon the basis of A.A. seniority, he tried to assume authority and rule the group. Failing in this, he broke their unity and later got drunk himself.

DAILY INVENTORY

Is A.A. run? Do our members rule? Where is A.A.'s authority? How is it expressed? Do we rule by force or lead by example?

SUGGESTED MEDITATION

A fellowship of sick persons, who are recovering from the effects of alcoholism, cannot be legislated back to health. They should be led by understanding alcoholics who have arrested their illness by 12 Step living and are willing to share their experiences with others. Our only authority is God's Will activating the conscience of our groups—His voice speaking through A.A. to the alcoholics who still suffer.

SPIRITUAL CONTACT

Our Father, may our examples of serenity and happy sobriety attract to us the alcoholics who still suffer. Make us realize the value of service.

DAILY PHYSICAL AUDIT

Good health is our best safeguard against disease. Some people inherit it while others must fight to acquire it. The alcoholic, regardless of his former status, has placed himself in the second category. Recovery from alcoholism now confronts us with two real problems. The first one is to regain our health. The second is to maintain it. Willingness to admit and treat our illness and physical defects is an important asset of recovery.

143

TWENTY-FIFTH DAILY REMINDER

Unity of purpose, thought and acts is vitally important to an A.A. group's success. Without unity we can only expect failure. You and I may stand or fall in accordance with the success of our group. We owe a unified stand on A.A. purpose to ourselves, to our group and to its future membership.

DAILY INVENTORY

Does the welfare of the group come first? Does individual recovery depend upon group unity? Who is responsible for the unity of the group?

SUGGESTED MEDITATION

Tradition One advises us that without unity an A.A. group cannot survive. Without a group many of us could not survive. Obviously, the preservation of group unity is the responsibility of every member. We must hang together or John

Barleycorn will surely hang us separately. With this in mind, let us put our petty ambitions aside and band ourselves together with determination to support the principles of A.A.

SPIRITUAL CONTACT

Our Father, we pray that our group may be unified in its purpose to maintain individual sobriety and to pass it on to alcoholics seeking our aid.

DAILY PHYSICAL AUDIT

Although the heart is innocent of creating many of the pains and feelings of discomfort attributed to it, we act wisely to investigate the cause of unusual symptoms which may occur. A good way to prevent heart trouble is to see your doctor for a check-up every year and to consult him at the appearance of any symptom which may or may not have its source in the heart. Perhaps this may disclose organic illness in time for treatment and cure.

145

TWENTY-SIXTH DAILY REMINDER

A dirty middle-aged alcoholic lay dying on an old couch in the slums of a midwestern city. Sick, helpless and broke he had called upon A.A. for help. Sympathetic members responded, placing him in a hospital. He recovered and later joined A.A. where he stayed and served with credit to his group.

DAILY INVENTORY

What are the requirements for A.A. membership? Are we interested in both low and high bottom drunks? How do we handle those who refuse to believe in God?

SUGGESTED MEDITATION

"The only requirement for membership is an honest desire to stop drinking." It is not within our province to refuse A.A. to an alcoholic who asks for help. God has a way of handling those who do not believe in Him. A.A. does not de-

mand belief in God, yet the newcomer soon learns that contented sobriety demands it. There can be no satisfactory personality change in a member who refuses spiritual help.

SPIRITUAL CONTACT

Our Father, prevent us from passing judgment upon anyone. Grant us wisdom to discern between tolerance and indulgence. Let us live and give A.A.

DAILY PHYSICAL AUDIT

Common sense governs the rules of healthful living. Good health does not result from a single act but is the result of many daily practices which eventually become habits of self-preservation. They keep us from "digging our grave with our teeth." There are detours to be observed on the road to Wellville which circumvent fast eating, overeating, gulping food down with liquids and eating when overfatigued.

147

TWENTY-SEVENTH DAILY REMINDER

An A.A. veteran, the main speaker at an anniversary meeting, sat waiting for almost two hours while other speakers dramatized many subjects — some of them foreign to A.A. Finally he was introduced. He spoke for thirty minutes, inspiring us with the humble virtues of A.A. His subject? Love and service.

DAILY INVENTORY

Have we ever visualized the power of true humility? Do we seek contented sobriety or A.A. recognition? Are our efforts inspired by love and service?

SUGGESTED MEDITATION

The truly great members of A.A. are all humble members. They give freely of their talent but seek no praise. The publicity seeker is different. He lacks humility and openly courts acclaim but never seems to feel small about it. We can be either great or small in A.A., but as we sacrifice our vanities upon the altar of A.A. service we will rise and grow in stature and gain recognition without seeking it.

SPIRITUAL CONTACT

Our Father, knowing the weakness of our vanity, we pray for the strength of humility. Reveal our need for love and service. Make us worthy A.A. servants.

DAILY PHYSICAL AUDIT

Alcohol does not contribute to diabetes, but diabetes can contribute to relapses. We find verification of this fact in the lives of our diabetics who, suffering from complications of their primary illness, go on a mental spree and end up drunk. A.A. diabetics have two incurable diseases to arrest. They should adhere strictly to their diet. Undue physical and mental effort must be avoided. Infection and neglect may lead to gangrene, blindness and death.

149

TWENTY-EIGHTH DAILY REMINDER

A few A.A. members and their wives were assembled at the home of another member for a weekly A.A. meeting. The host arrived too late to hold his meeting. When questioned about his absence he shouted, "What in h - - l is all this bellyaching about — I'm here and sober, isn't that enough?"

DAILY INVENTORY

Is sullen and surly sobriety enough? How far off the beam dare we get? Is it possible to benefit from or add to A.A. meetings in an angry, sullen mood?

SUGGESTED MEDITATION

It is remarkable that a few months of sobriety will allow us to forget that the mental binge always precedes the physical drunk. Members who are physically dry and mentally wet do not stay that way. We must either improve our sobri-

ety or vainly try to suppress our alcoholism. Suppression is not our answer. It only leads to drinking. It lets us drift back, like washed pigs, to wallow in the alcoholic mire.

SPIRITUAL CONTACT

Our Father, help us to stay put with our group. Fill us with enthusiasm for the A.A. program. We pray for willingness to improve upon our sobriety.

DAILY PHYSICAL AUDIT

Relaxation and sleep are not only good health practices, they are vital essentials of life itself. We cannot miss them for any great length of time and live healthy lives. Nature's rules for the upkeep of the body are definite and exacting. Alcoholics require systematic daily rest periods to relieve mental fatigue. Our body tissues need sleep to overcome the chemical changes caused by work during the day.

151

TWENTY-NINTH DAILY REMINDER

An older A.A. member killed himself today, bringing sorrow and grave concern to the members of his group. Despite their knowledge of infidelity with his family, self-sedation and his refusal to consider alcoholism a disease, some members wondered why he resumed drinking and then took his own life.

DAILY INVENTORY

The reasons for this man's troubles are well defined in Chapter Five in the Big Book. Honesty pays big dividends in A.A. Let's work it 24 hours daily.

SUGGESTED MEDITATION

All drinking alcoholics are potential suicides. Contented sobriety and A.A. are not compatible with suicide, nor with dishonesty in business and home dealings, nor in sneaking that first drink. Alcoholism is more than sin—it is sickness also.

If it were just a sinful act we could re-cover by asking forgiveness and keep right on drinking. That's what we did be-fore A.A. That's what killed our old friend.

SPIRITUAL CONTACT

Our Father, we know our great need for Your help and wisdom. Grant them to us. Enable us to arrest the dishonesty and fatality of alcoholism.

DAILY PHYSICAL AUDIT

Medical doctors have not recognized alcohol as the cause of gastric ulcer. Alcohol, smoking and spicy foods, however, do aggravate conditions where ulcers exist. Members with known ulcers are advised to follow prescribed medication and diet. Persons with high-up abdominal pains, bloating, pains in the back, nausea after eating and black or bloody stools may be developing ulcers and should get a physical checkup.

THIRTIETH DAILY REMINDER

The unmanageable lives which we have developed from years of self-centered drinking have taught us our weakness apart from the help and influence of a Higher Power. A.A. suggests that we avail ourselves of God's power. It advises us to pray unselfish prayers that help us and are a blessing to mankind.

DAILY INVENTORY

Have we a relationship with God? Is there a brotherhood of man? Are we our brother's keeper? Do we understand the power of unselfish prayer?

SUGGESTED MEDITATION

Some members claim that A.A. is a selfish program. Is this true or is A.A. just the opposite—a program which frees us from self-centeredness? Their statements are well meant but most mislead-

ing. It seems that intelligence, not selfishness, actuates our recovery from alcoholism. Step 11 suggests that we pray to lose self-will and that our prayers include the welfare of others.

SPIRITUAL CONTACT

Our Father, let us see beyond life's material needs to our 24-hour spiritual needs. Clear our minds of selfishness. May we be guided by Your Will.

DAILY PHYSICAL AUDIT

Most alcoholics require some form of moderate exercise to keep fit physically. Since ignorance of the harm of overexertion does not shield us from its physical penalties, we should work within the individual limits of our strength. Outdoor exercise taken once or twice a week stimulates circulation, helps digestion, aids elimination and adds years to our lives.

THIRTY-FIRST DAILY REMINDER

An A.A. founder once said, with reference to a vital phase of spiritual recovery, "What others think about you is never as important as what you think about them." A.A. character cannot be concealed. By the rule of attraction it draws to itself of its own kind. Spiritual growth operates by this rule.

DAILY INVENTORY

What thoughts are we giving to the discipline of our emotions? Do we realize that they can either "make or break us"? We should check this angle.

SUGGESTED MEDITATION

Straight intellectual knowledge cannot improve our A.A. personality. But honest daily effort to "live and let live" gives us character and provides examples of contented sobriety which are important to us. Our treatment of others decides their attitude toward us. After physical recovery, our sobriety depends largely upon how we discipline our emotions and live the A.A. program—not from just knowing it.

SPIRITUAL CONTACT

Our Father, we pray for emotional maturity. Help us to discipline our emotional energy. Grant us the wisdom and the power to live sober, happy lives.

DAILY PHYSICAL AUDIT

Good health is man's most prized possession. But like other phases of his recovery the alcoholic must earn it. Physical vitality should not be abused. It tends to degenerate rapidly when denied fresh air, sunshine, exercise, proper food and sufficient rest. The road to good health lies not in occasional access to these requisites of life but in their regular use.

"LIVE AND LET LIVE"

Few alcoholics come into A.A. with the voluntary purpose of staying drunk. Yet, some burdened with resentment and dominated by self-centered objectives, continue to drink. Even though A.A. provides a solution for their alcoholic dilemma, not all will accept it.

Recovery is possible for those who will live the A.A. program to arrest their alcoholism. But, even for them, there is a battle to be won. Rebellious alcoholic personalities die hard. Hence, the reason for our progressive 24-hour program to sublimate our thinking so that by being honest with ourselves we may deal fairly and decently with others.

The old adage "live and let live" is a basic principle of our recovery program. We can detect its influence in every step. Our thoughts regarding others and the manner in which we treat them are so important to our recovery that they often sway the balance between success and failure. We maintain the miracle of our sobriety by sharing it with other alcoholics. To hoard our good fortune is to lose it.

A.A. is not a theory. It is a way of sober, normal living. We live it successfully when we admit our alcoholism and seek recovery. We gain forgiveness when we become forgiving. We escape suffering and punishment when we stop dealing it out. We acquire sobriety and peace of mind when we start living the 12 Steps on the basis of love and service — prompted only by a desire to live and let live.

HBS-2

USD $17.95   CAD $24.95

ISBN: 978-0-89486-027-0

Order No. 1040